AMZ

10/2020

D1208846

We all belong

Goss
CASTLE

Goss Castle
Copyright 2020
All rights reserved
3rd edition

DEDICATION

For everyone

ACKNOWLEDGEMENTS

Illustrator / author: Nathalie Goss
Author / editor: Alex Goss

instagram.com/nathaliegossdesigns

If you look closely, you'll soon see,

no one looks the same as me.

I have lovely dark **curly** hair...

and my hair is straight,

long

and fair.

I am **tall**

I am **small**

We both love

to play football.

I like to be **loud!**

I'm sometimes **shy**...

Who is smart?

You and I

Everyone is different in one way or another.

I even look different to my sister and my brother.

Some might say we're a different race.

We think that's completely

ace!

What is our race?

Is it the colour of our skin?

It means we share one kind of thing.

Sharing what?

Sharing looks.

Sharing things in history books.

HISTORY

We're the same in some ways too.

We like **dancing!**

We like

blue!

We both like **red**.

We both are kind.

We both like reading

to unwind.

My eyes are **brown**

My eyes are **blue**

When we come together

There's nothing we can't do

It'd be boring if we all looked the same.

If we ate the same food.

If we had the same names.

My family and I eat rice and peas.

That sounds nice, can I try that please?

My family sing precious

songs

My family wear nice

sarongs

In our school

we **all** belong...

Together we all get along!

I love my language and the way I speak.

I love my home.

I love my street.

Where I live, the animals squark.

Near my home, we go for walks.

HOME
HOME

Not one of us are out of place.

We all belong to the

human race

Can you draw yourself and a friend?

In what ways are you the same?

In what ways are you different?

You are both **amazing!**

Also available from Goss Castle

Your reviews help us get more kids learning through reading.

Please share your feedback. We read every one!

1. **Go to Amazon**
2. **Click Orders**
3. **Find the book and click** Write a Product Review

Goss
CASTLE

Made in the USA
Columbia, SC
30 September 2020